THIS WHERE'S WALLY? BOOK BELONGS TO:

HEY, WALLY FANS! FIVE INTREPID TRAVELLERS
ARE LOST IN EVERY SCENE! CAN YOU FIND THEM?

ODLAW   WIZARD
          WHITEBEARD   WENDA   WOOF   WALLY

AND IN EVERY SCENE, THE TRAVELLERS
HAVE EACH LOST SOMETHING PRECIOUS!
CAN YOU FIND THEM TOO?

WALLY'S KEY   WOOF'S BONE   WENDA'S CAMERA

WIZARD WHITEBEARD'S SCROLL   ODLAW'S BINOCULARS

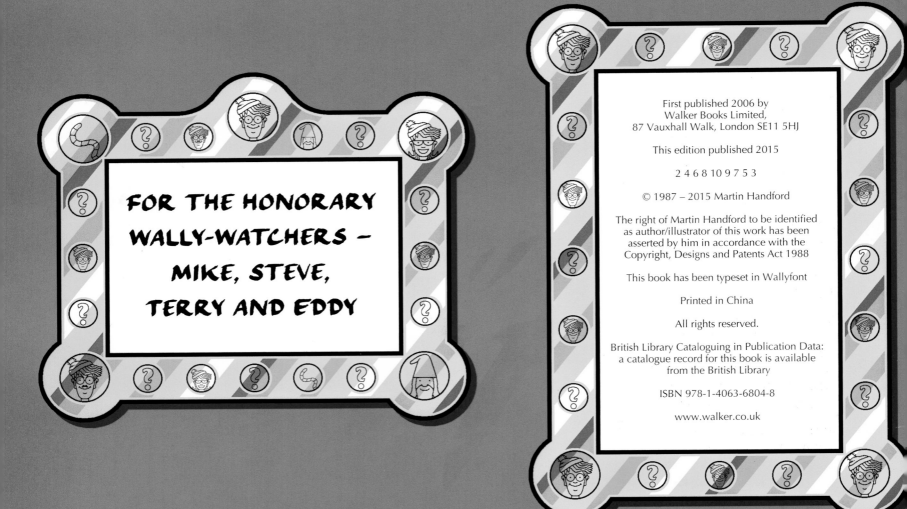

FOR THE HONORARY
WALLY-WATCHERS –
MIKE, STEVE,
TERRY AND EDDY

First published 2006 by
Walker Books Limited,
87 Vauxhall Walk, London SE11 5HJ

This edition published 2015

2 4 6 8 10 9 7 5 3

© 1987 – 2015 Martin Handford

The right of Martin Handford to be identified
as author/illustrator of this work has been
asserted by him in accordance with the
Copyright, Designs and Patents Act 1988

This book has been typeset in Wallyfont

Printed in China

All rights reserved.

British Library Cataloguing in Publication Data:
a catalogue record for this book is available
from the British Library

ISBN 978-1-4063-6804-8

www.walker.co.uk

THE GREAT PICTURE HUNT

HEY, WALLY FANS, WELCOME TO THE GREAT PICTURE HUNT!

THE FUN STARTS IN EXHIBIT 1, ODLAW'S PICTURE PANDEMONIUM, WHERE YOU'LL FIND 30 ENORMOUS PORTRAITS. WOW! EXAMINE THEM CAREFULLY, BECAUSE EVERY ONE OF THE PORTRAIT SUBJECTS CAN BE FOUND SOMEWHERE ELSE IN THIS BOOK ... BUT ONLY ONCE. YOUR CHALLENGE IS TO FIND THESE SLIPPERY SUBJECTS WHEREVER THEY MIGHT BE HIDING.

BUT THE FUN DOESN'T STOP THERE. LOOK OUT FOR THE SPOT-THE-DIFFERENCE PUZZLES, MATCHING GAMES, AND THE CHALLENGING CHECKLISTS WITH MORE THINGS TO SPOT FOR EXTRA WALLY-WATCHING CREDIT. FANTASTIC!

AND NOW, GALLERY GAZERS, LET THE GREAT PICTURE HUNT BEGIN!

Wally

AND, OF COURSE, OUR FRAME GAME APART, THERE ARE FIVE INTREPID PORTRAITEERS TO FIND IN EVERY SCENE...

FIND WALLY ... OUR YOUNG GALLERY GUIDE, WHO TRAVELS EVERYWHERE!
FIND WOOF ... WHO WAGS HIS NOT-SO-BRUSH-LIKE TAIL (WHICH IS ALL YOU CAN SEE!).
FIND WENDA ... WHO TAKES THE PICTURES (BUT DOESN'T PAINT THEM!).
FIND WIZARD WHITEBEARD ... THE OLD MASTER WHO CASTS COLOURFUL SPELLS!
FIND ODLAW ... WHO'S BEEN AN EXHIBIT IN MANY A ROGUES' GALLERY!

AND NOT FORGETTING MY LOST KEY, WENDA'S MISPLACED CAMERA, WOOF'S MISSING BONE, WIZARD WHITEBEARD'S MISLAID SCROLL AND ODLAW'S ABSENT BINOCULARS...

EXHIBIT 1 – ODLAW'S PICTURE PANDEMONIUM

WOW, WALLY FANS, WHAT A PANDEMONIUM! HAVE YOU EVER SEEN SO MANY YELLOW-AND-BLACK STRIPES IN ONE PLACE? AMAZING! WE'RE HERE IN ODLAW'S PICTURE GALLERY AND JUST LOOK AT WHAT HIS ARTFUL ASSOCIATES HAVE BROUGHT WITH THEM – 30 PECULIAR PORTRAITS IN AN ODDITY OF FRAMES. AMAZING! THERE'S QUITE A CAST OF CHARACTERS IN THESE PAINTINGS, AND THEY ALL APPEAR AGAIN ELSEWHERE IN THE BOOK. AND PICTURE THIS – ONE OF THEM EVEN APPEARS SOMEWHERE IN THIS CRAZY CROWD! SO PATIENTLY PERUSE THE PICTURE UNTIL YOU FIND HIM. GOOD LUCK WHEREVER YOU LOOK IN YOUR HUNT FOR THE PLACES WITH THE FACES! WHAT A PICTURE!

EXHIBIT 2 —
A SPORTING LIFE

WELCOME, PICTURE HUNT PALS, TO MY
SPECIAL REPORT FROM THE LAND OF
SPORT. FANTASTIC! IT'S LIKE THE OLYMPICS
EVERY DAY HERE, BUT WITH SO MANY ATHLETIC
EVENTS ON THE MENU THERE'S NO TIME LEFT
FOR ANY REST AND RELAXATION. HOWEVER
THERE'S NOTHING TOO STRENUOUS ABOUT
OUR MAIN EVENT, THE GREAT PICTURE
HUNT, SO KEEP YOUR EYES ON THE BALL
AND HAVE YOUR POINTER FINGERS
READY. ON YOUR MARKS,
GET SET, GO!

EXHIBIT 5 – THE PINK PARADISE PARTY

IT'S SATURDAY NIGHT, THE TEMPERATURE IS RISING AND IT LOOKS AS IF A RASH OF MUSICAL MAYHEM AND DISCO FEVER HAS BROKEN OUT IN THIS DIZZY DANCE HALL. WOW! AMAZING! HIP HIP-HOPPERS, BODY-POPPERS, ROCK-AND-ROLLERS AND BODY-AND-SOULERS – IT'S A PACKED-OUT, PARTYGOERS' PINK PARADISE. SO GET ON DOWN, CUT YOUR GROOVE AND MAKE YOUR MOVES – IT'S TIME TO SHUFFLE YOUR FEET TO THE PICTURE HUNT BEAT!

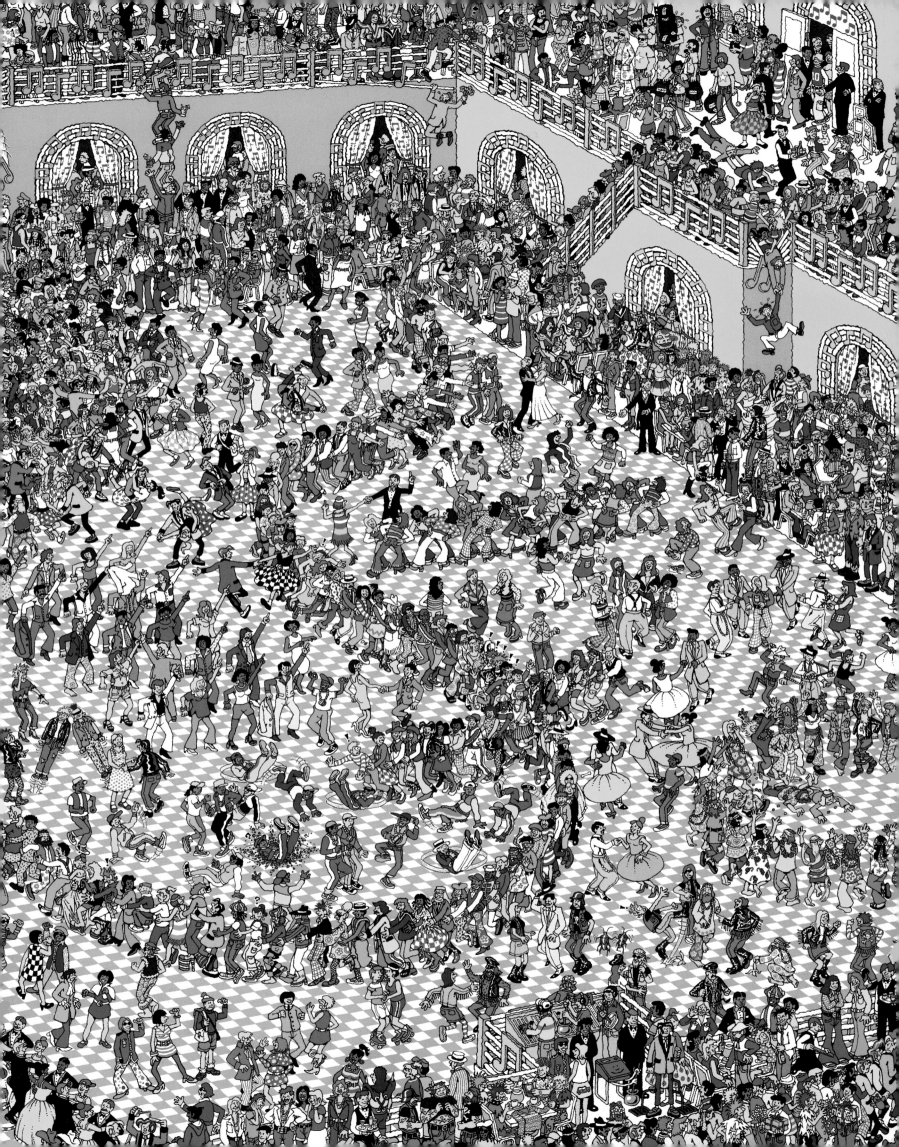

EXHIBIT 6 – OLD FRIENDS

AH, PICTURE HUNT PALS, HOW I LOVE TO LOOK THROUGH MY
SCRAPBOOKS OF MEMORIES AND SOUVENIRS. THIS PAGE IS
ONE OF MY FAVOURITES: A COLLAGE CRAMMED WITH FAMILIAR
FACES FROM MY EARLIER ADVENTURES. FANTASTIC! EVEN THE
MOST DEDICATED OF WALLY WATCHERS AMONGST YOU WILL
HAVE TROUBLE RECOGNIZING ALL OF THE OLD FRIENDS HERE,
IT'S QUITE A CHALLENGE. BUT HERE'S AN EASIER TEASER
THAT ANYONE CAN DO: JUST LOOK AT ALL THE CIRCLED
FACES IN THIS FRAME, THEN SEE IF YOU CAN SPOT THEM
IN THE SURROUNDING PICTURE.

EXHIBIT 7 – OLD FRIENDS AGAIN

IT'S ALWAYS NICE WHEN FRIENDS CAN STAY FOR A LITTLE LONGER... I'VE CALLED THIS "OLD FRIENDS AGAIN" BECAUSE THAT'S EXACTLY WHAT IT IS ... A FRAMED COLLECTION OF SOME OF THE OLD FRIENDS FROM THE PICTURE NEXT DOOR, BUT IN SILHOUETTE FORM. AND JUST TO MAKE IT A BIT MORE INTERESTING, SOME OF THEM ARE PICTURED UPSIDE DOWN OR SIDEWAYS. CAN YOU MATCH EACH SILHOUETTE HERE WITH THE CORRECT OLD FRIEND IN EXHIBIT 6? SO, ONWARDS AND UPWARDS (AND DOWNWARDS AND SIDEWAYS), MY PICTURE HUNT PORTRAITEERS!

EXHIBIT 8 – THE MONSTER MASTERPIECE

YIKES, SPIKES AND KNOBBLY BITS, I'M LOST IN THE LAND OF THE MONSTERS. WOW! WHAT A CREATURE FEATURE! WHO'S IN CHARGE HERE, ANYWAY? THE HELMETED HUNTERS OR THEIR QUARRELSOME QUARRY? BUT DON'T BE PUT OFF BY THIS MONSTER MAYHEM, ART FANS, PLAY ON WITH THE PUZZLE, THERE ARE STILL SOME PORTRAIT SUBJECTS TO FIND. WHAT A MONSTROSITY!

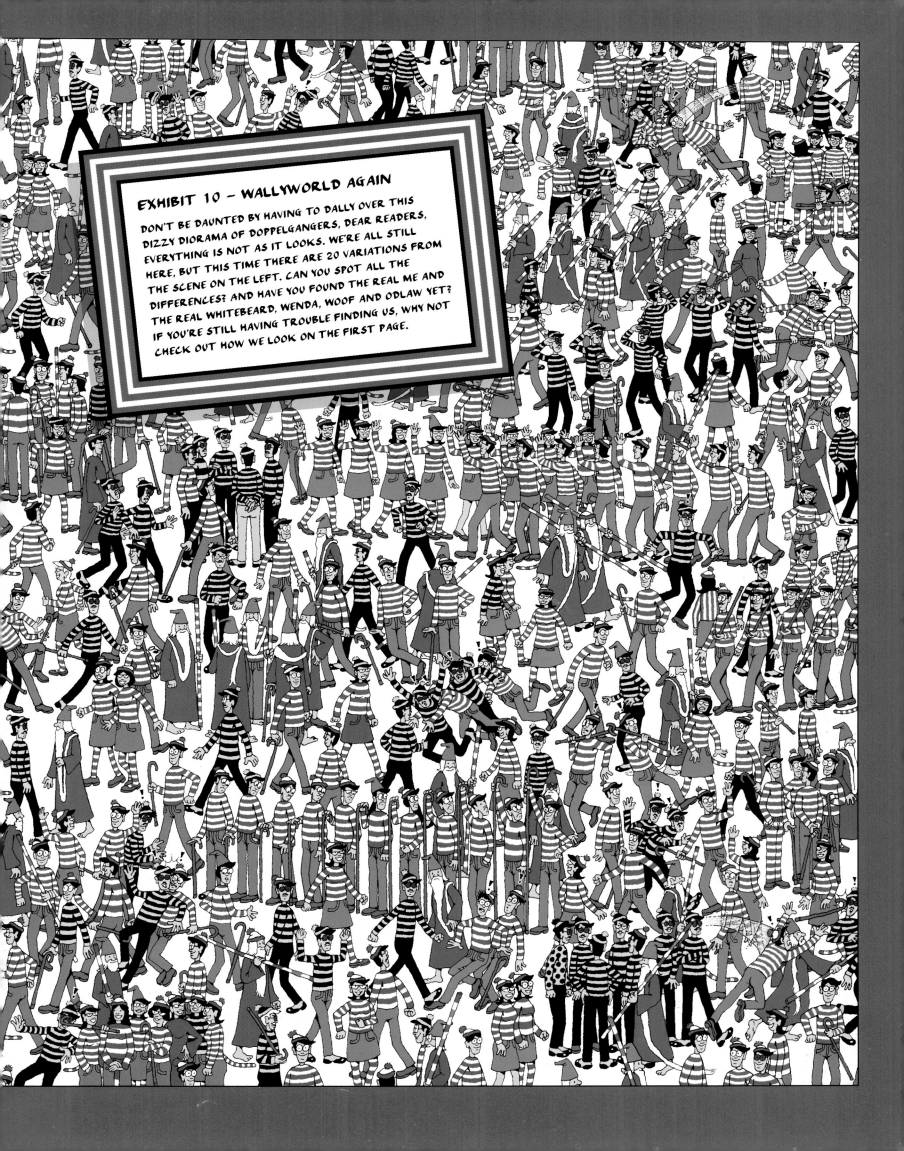

EXHIBIT 10 – WALLYWORLD AGAIN

DON'T BE DAUNTED BY HAVING TO DALLY OVER THIS
DIZZY DIORAMA OF DOPPELGANGERS, DEAR READERS,
EVERYTHING IS NOT AS IT LOOKS. WE'RE ALL STILL
HERE, BUT THIS TIME THERE ARE 20 VARIATIONS FROM
THE SCENE ON THE LEFT. CAN YOU SPOT ALL THE
DIFFERENCES? AND HAVE YOU FOUND THE REAL ME AND
THE REAL WHITEBEARD, WENDA, WOOF AND ODLAW YET?
IF YOU'RE STILL HAVING TROUBLE FINDING US, WHY NOT
CHECK OUT HOW WE LOOK ON THE FIRST PAGE.

EXHIBIT 11 – PIRATE PANORAMA

SHIVER ME TIMBERS, SHIPMATES, WHAT PERFIDIOUS, PIRATE PANORAMA IS THIS? WOW! AMAZING! I'VE SAILED THE SEVEN SEAS SEARCHING FOR THESE 30 PORTRAIT PEOPLE, AND NOW THAT OUR JOURNEY IS ALMOST OVER, I JUST HOPE THE PIRATES DON'T MAKE THEM WALK THE PLANK! I'M SURE THOSE FARAWAY CASTAWAYS WOULD PREFER TO BE MAROONED ON A DESERT ISLAND THAN TO MEET THESE BARMY BUCCANEERS. ALL HANDS ON DECK!

EXHIBIT 12 – THE GREAT PORTRAIT EXHIBITION

OUR JOURNEY IS NOW OVER, PORTRAIT PERUSERS, BUT WHAT A FITTING FINALE: A FANTASTIC EXHIBITION IN A PROPER ART GALLERY. WOW! AMAZING! THE CROWD HERE SEEMS MUCH MORE WELCOMING THAN ODLAW'S ODD ENSEMBLE. I'M ALSO REALLY PLEASED THAT ALL 30 OF THE CHARACTERS WE'VE BEEN HUNTING FOR ARE HERE AMONGST THE GALLERY GAZERS. SEE IF YOU CAN SPOT THEM AS THEY WANDER FREELY AMONG THE VISITORS ENJOYING THE SHOW. I HOPE YOU FOUND THEM IN THE PREVIOUS PAGES, TOO. IF NOT, THERE'S STILL PLENTY OF TIME TO DO SO – THE EXHIBITION NEVER CLOSES. HAPPY HUNTING!

WHERE'S WALLY?

THE GREAT PICTURE HUNT!

CHECKLISTS & ANSWERS

Lots more things for Wally watchers to look for!

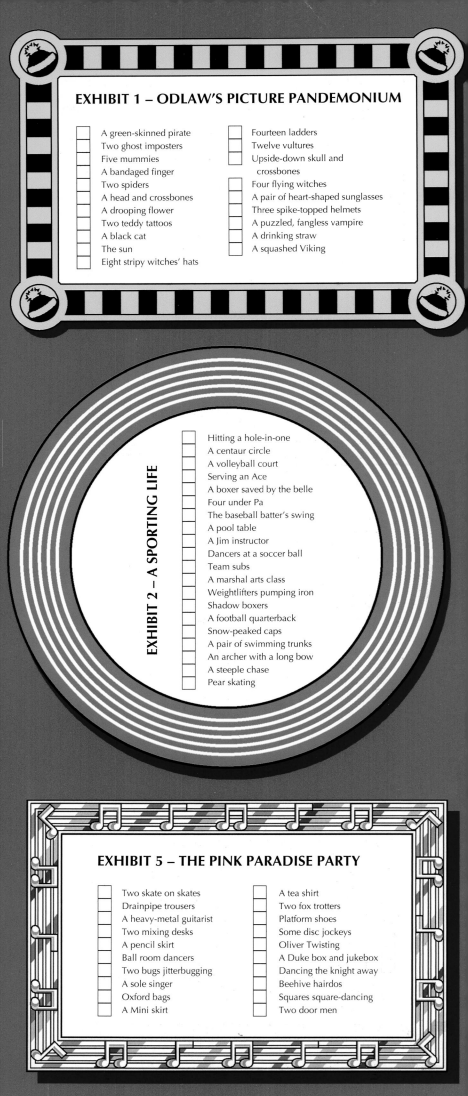

EXHIBIT 1 – ODLAW'S PICTURE PANDEMONIUM

- A green-skinned pirate
- Two ghost imposters
- Five mummies
- A bandaged finger
- Two spiders
- A head and crossbones
- A drooping flower
- Two teddy tattoos
- A black cat
- The sun
- Eight stripy witches' hats
- Fourteen ladders
- Twelve vultures
- Upside-down skull and crossbones
- Four flying witches
- A pair of heart-shaped sunglasses
- Three spike-topped helmets
- A puzzled, fangless vampire
- A drinking straw
- A squashed Viking

EXHIBIT 2 – A SPORTING LIFE

- Hitting a hole-in-one
- A centaur circle
- A volleyball court
- Serving an Ace
- A boxer saved by the belle
- Four under Pa
- The baseball batter's swing
- A pool table
- A Jim instructor
- Dancers at a soccer ball
- Team subs
- A marshal arts class
- Weightlifters pumping iron
- Shadow boxers
- A football quarterback
- Snow-peaked caps
- A pair of swimming trunks
- An archer with a long bow
- A steeple chase
- Pear skating

EXHIBIT 5 – THE PINK PARADISE PARTY

- Two skate on skates
- Drainpipe trousers
- A heavy-metal guitarist
- Two mixing desks
- A pencil skirt
- Ball room dancers
- Two bugs jitterbugging
- A sole singer
- Oxford bags
- A Mini skirt
- A tea shirt
- Two fox trotters
- Platform shoes
- Some disc jockeys
- Oliver Twisting
- A Duke box and jukebox
- Dancing the knight away
- Beehive hairdos
- Squares square-dancing
- Two door men

SPOT THE DIFFERENCE
EXHIBIT 4 –
BROWN SAILORS & GREEN SCALERS AGAIN
DID YOU SPOT THESE?

- A missing tail-end
- An absent cloud
- A brown balloon
- A balloon number missing
- A missing tooth
- A missing lasso
- Some missing smoke
- A missing flag
- A monster without spots
- A back-to-front number
- A missing flag number
- A missing monster
- An absent sailor
- A missing telescope
- A man with a yellow beard
- Some missing green slime
- An extra sailor
- A slime gun without a nozzle
- A brown sea-creature
- A sailor in a white top

EXHIBIT 6 – OLD FRIENDS

- A lady in a blue ball gown
- A snowman
- A monster in a man-suit
- A red astronaut
- A woman with a green bag
- A pirate surfing
- A thirsty boy
- A cook with a dough nut
- A crab clipping a toenail
- A hippo with a jumbo-sized toothbrush
- A pole vaulter taking a break
- A rude statue
- A bull frog
- A man holding a flower
- A man in a manhole
- A horse-drawn wagon
- A woman with a clipboard
- A swimmer in shades
- A dog in the shade
- A woman holding a hairbrush

EXHIBIT 8 – THE MONSTER MASTERPIECE

- Salt and pepper pots
- A ropey snake bite
- A monster wearing a napkin
- A tail lassoing a foot
- Two hunters using hankies
- A raft made from snakes
- A ticklish monster
- A snake tripping up hunters
- A pointed helmet prodding a hunter
- A monster munching timber
- One round shield
- Six arrows rebounding off monsters
- A swimming race
- A bunch of flowers
- A log stuck on a horn
- A monster wielding three swords
- A hunter held upside down
- A long tongue lassoing a leg
- A monster chewing spears
- Two hunter boys sliding

EXHIBIT 11 – PIRATE PANORAMA

- Seven bottles
- Diving boards
- A massage in a bottle
- A giant wave
- A school of whales
- A pirate riding the serf
- Five birds
- A deck of cards
- Seven flags
- A pirate walking the plank
- A dessert island
- Eleven cannons
- The deep blue C
- Eight fins
- A pirate with an axe and a cutlass
- A tap
- Lobster beds
- Four cannonballs
- A two-foot gun barrel
- Two coloured patches

SPOT THE DIFFERENCE
EXHIBIT 10 – WALLYWORLD AGAIN
DID YOU SPOT THESE?

- A Wenda wearing a red skirt
- A Whitebeard wearing a red hat
- A Wally whose stripes have shifted
- A Whitebeard whose staff is missing
- A hat that has lost its bobble
- A Wally in stripy trousers
- A Wenda who has lost her glasses
- A Woof with a longer tail
- A missing walking stick
- A spotty Odlaw
- A missing wizard
- A Wally no longer smiling
- A missing Woof's tail
- An Odlaw missing a hat
- An Odlaw wearing different glasses
- A Wenda in blue-and-white tights
- A walking stick missing a tip
- An Odlaw in yellow trousers
- A Wenda with vertical stripes
- A wizard beard that has changed colour

EXHIBIT 12 – THE GREAT PICTURE EXHIBITION

- Nineteen flowers
- A woman guitarist
- A leaking-water colour
- Two duelling artists
- Eleven horses
- Four brooms
- An empty red frame
- Two cavewomen
- A very long white beard
- Nine fish
- An artist with seven brushes
- A grey donkey
- A rude shield
- Two brushes in a hatband
- A hungry wolf
- A red bow tie
- An artist with a big brush
- Five stools
- Stripy red-and-yellow sleeves
- A cracked vase

AND JUST ONE MORE THING…

Why not brush up on your maths with this sum?
Add the number of frames containing pictures of men in
Exhibit 1 to the number of blue picture frames in Exhibit 7.
Then subtract the number of triangular frames in Exhibit 12.